# Handbook of Intuitive Intelligenceπ™ for Entrepreneurs: Knowing the Secret Key to Success

*Strategies to count on when it really counts!*

DR. MANJ SUBIAH

Disclaimer

This book has been written to provide information about Intuitive Intelligence∏™. While every effort has been made to make this information as complete and accurate as possible, the author is not responsible for any errors in typography or content. This book contains information on Intuitive Intelligence∏™ only up to the publishing date. Therefore, the purpose of this book is to serve as a guide – not as the ultimate source of information on the topic. While the purpose of this book is also to educate, the author does not warrant that the information contained in this book is fully complete and shall not be responsible for any errors or omissions. The author shall have neither liability nor responsibility to any person or entity with respect to any loss or damage caused or alleged to be caused directly or indirectly by this book.

ISBN-13: 978-1530591503

ISBN-10: 1530591503

# DEDICATION

To my husband Cyril and my daughter Suria Devi, you have both taught me a love that is truly timeless.

My heartfelt gratitude to my family, friends and all those people who have been my teachers, knowingly and unknowingly on the path to the discovery of Intuitive Intelligence∏™.

This book is also dedicated to my extraordinary Mentors and those brave, intrepid, Entrepreneur - warriors doing daily battle, out there.

Other books by Dr Manj Subiah


Book of 365 Meditations: Awaken your Intuitive IntelligenceΠ™!

In progress:
Handbook of Intuitive IntelligenceΠ™ for Leaders
Handbook of Intuitive IntelligenceΠ™ for Managers
Handbook of Intuitive IntelligenceΠ™ for Parents
Handbook of Intuitive IntelligenceΠ™ for Children

GIIS: Transforming People and Planet for Better
P.O. Box 145252
Brackengardens
http://www.giis.co.za

# CONTENTS

# WITH GRATEFUL ACKNOWLEDGEMENT

Thank you to Bhagavan Sri Ramana Maharshi, and the Master Mind for teaching me how to listen to the infallible wisdom of Intuitive Intelligence∏™. To you, I owe the ultimate debt.

Special thanks to my extraordinary mentor Blair Singer, and all the amazing Master Facilitators I met in the USA in November 2015. You know, without you, this book would not have seen the light of day.

Massive thanks to my mentors, mentees, friends and colleagues who have never failed to inspire me along the way: Anil Singal, Brenda Kali, Brian Walsh, Charlotte Mosely, Cherie Blair Mentoring Women in Business Executive, Charlotte Wong, Cristal Peterson, Des and Belinda Werner, Francis Cholle, Gianluca Dedonno, John Shehata, Jayne Johnson, Jill Wright, Kuda Makuzwa, Kurly Marwaha, Marta Valente, Nancy Mavunga, Rob King, Robin Banks, Roger Hamilton, Russel Brunson, Swamini Krishnapriyananda, Drs. Hendrik Cronje, John Demartini, Sidney and Estelle Shipham, Ria Marshall, Vladimir Bacvanski, Professors Anton Grobler, Peet Venter and Stella Nkomo.

# FOREWORD BY BLAIR SINGER

As an entrepreneur or leader, have you ever been faced with these decisions: "Do I invest or not?" "Is this person going to be a good partner or not?" "Should I pull the trigger on this deal or not?" "I have a nagging feeling about this transaction….why?"

These are questions that entrepreneurs and leaders face every day. There are secondary questions as well: "Should I follow a logical process or trust my gut?" "Is my gut feeling really dependable or is it just my reactive emotions kicking up?"

When I look back on some of the pivotal decisions I have made in my life, they include moments in business, in my family and in my own personal growth. In retrospect, there were some good ones and some questionable ones. However, I know that with many of the dubious decisions, I can very often recall that I second guessed myself in those situations. I am sure that you know the feeling.

It's a moment where there may be little preparation, scant advance notice, but a time when you must react. It is a moment where a bigger part of me said "A" and another little voice in my head said "B". Unfortunately many of those moments, you never get back.

So where does the first thought come from? That one

that leads to bigger and better outcomes.  What if there was a way to develop your own intelligence to the degree that you could tap into that amazing intuitive wisdom on a consistent basis?

Dr Manj Subiah's groundbreaking work has discovered how you can access your own intuitive intelligence∏™ in order to be in the right place at the right time, doing the right things.

In business, the difference between a good decision and a bad one can mean either making millions or struggling in tedious mediocrity for years.  In relationships, it can mean a life of bliss or frustration.  And by the way, intuitive intelligence∏™ is not just about "major decisions."  It's every move you make.  I have worked with hundreds of thousands of leaders and entrepreneurs all over the world for over twenty-five years.  The unfortunate fact is most entrepreneurs fail in business.  The ones that get back up and succeed are those who have developed supreme confidence and clarity.

Dr Manj's work not only supports you tapping into that infinite clarity that you possess, but teaches you to ultimately trust yourself, which will give you the peace of mind, confidence and optimism you need to truly go the distance to achieve your dreams.

***Blair Singer*** : Entrepreneur, Author: SalesDogs®, Team Code of Honor and Little Voice Mastery, Rich Dad Advisor to Robert Kiyosaki.

# PREFACE

Somewhat despite my reservations, this book has taken on a surprisingly non-academic style, partly due perhaps, to the question of, 'How else does one give voice to living an intuitively intelligent life?' I have no succinct answer here, except to say that I have found no separation in business, professional and personal, when it comes to accessing Intuitive Intelligence∏™. Practically speaking, a unique construct such as this, deserves contextual distinction; hence the form of reference – 'Intuitive Intelligence∏™.' This is an inimitable ability you have on call to serve you 24/7, whether you know it or not.

I remember still, the dark days of studying for my doctorate, trying to unravel bit by bit, the existence of Intuitive Intelligence∏™ and encountering plenty of resistance along the way. The battle it seemed, was not so much in finding evidence of this unseen force out in the field, but in dealing with the range of positive and negative reactions from members of the respected academic community. Those responses ranged from, 'This is crucial for leaders, but be aware - this is a difficult topic', to a somewhat less appreciative '...bah, bullsh*t!'

Perhaps the only reason I persevered, was through the support of great mentors and extraordinary leaders who knew enough about what worked in business to bear testimony to Intuitive Intelligence∏™. On reflection, I realise now that, given the connective nature of Intuitive Intelligence∏™, any capitulation from me meant that someone else would take on the task and see it through.

The simple truth is that, to those willing to listen, Intuitive Intelligence∏™ speaks - albeit in silence - but it speaks nonetheless. So, persevere I did. Eventually in 2013, a thirty year old preoccupation with Intuitive Intelligence∏™ culminated in the award of a business doctorate, acknowledging the role of Intuitive Intelligence∏™ in business leaders. The implications were far reaching. Why?

Well, it's like this. For so long we were blind to the existence of dark matter, and now for the first time, it seems we are able to take a peek under the cosmic hood to see a deep seated intelligence at work in the universe. An intelligence which is in synch with the cosmos, and in the case of intuitive intelligence∏™, one which seems bent on using man as its' motherboard.

So, I've come to see that to acknowledge the existence of Intuitive Intelligence∏™ is to unlock one of the ways in which consciousness transitions from pure quantum potential to physical manifested reality.

On a personal front, the pure promise of Intuitive Intelligence∏™ is that you develop an ability not just to make effective decisions, but to access an ever present wisdom anytime, anyplace. By using the processes, tools and techniques in this handbook, you will find that you are able to stand grounded in your greatness of being; as strong within as you are without. The gift of being yourself, just as you are....

So, you may use this handbook as a 'dive in' take on Intuitive Intelligence∏™ and properly immerse yourself, or; you may choose to cautiously dip your toe into it bit by bit; making notes as you go along, building your skills with daily practice. Either way, this condensed version, absorbed one chapter at a time starts to unfold, create and manifest in your own life. You will soon know, exquisitely, for yourself; that your Intuitive Intelligence∏™ is present and that you can acknowledge its' hand in the amazing events and connections happening in your life. To develop your Intuitive Intelligence∏™ further, use the links and resources given in this book.

**Why this book now?**

The moment is etched on my mind forever. It is Friday, 13th November 2015, in Phoenix, Arizona, USA. I receive a standing ovation from the audience of Blair Singers' Master Facilitators Programme. I had just finished presenting an excerpt of the Intuitive Intelligence∏™ programme to them. Standing there on stage looking at the faces before me, some of them wet with tears - as tear streaked as my own, the moment seemed to be one where I was a witness, rather than a participant. In that whirling blur, I heard my mentor and facilitator, Blair Singer say 'By doing this, do you see how you've allowed them to go there?' He was referring to how the audience had responded to the message of Intuitive Intelligence∏™. They had made a connection to a place deep inside themselves and the resonance was palpable in the room. It all happened at such a subtle, wordless level, that I felt myself reach a turning point. I knew then that this book had to be written. No more procrastination. No matter whether I felt ready or not, this was no longer about me. I had to take the value and message of Intuitive Intelligence∏™ out to others...*now. No more delays - it was crunch time.*

Prior to that moment of truth, the concept of this book had been pretty comfortable, living inside my head, minding its' own business, but that defining moment changed everything. I realised the message of Intuitive Intelligence∏™, in a strife torn world, was long overdue... And then a strange thing happened. I began to notice, in the weeks that followed, how this book would write itself whenever I learnt to get out of my own way. So then, the book finally emerged in the shape of simply showcasing Intuitive Intelligence∏™ to the world. Just what it is, *as it is*.

The message of Intuitive Intelligence∏™ etched from the actions of entrepreneurs, is always present in one form or another. In fact, it is present whenever man reaches out beyond himself to eke out right action.

Whenever entrepreneurs and leaders stretch themselves beyond their bounded limits, such right action, often beyond expectation, shows the evidence of how one can tell the trail and trace of Intuitive Intelligence∏™. Before now, the open acknowledgement of Intuitive Intelligence∏™ was always something I thought would only happen in the far-off future, like the writing of a memoir. But after decision day, it was something I simply had to *'let happen...'*

It was *deed de-facto* then, that I would, by virtue of this book, be prompted to seek, find and acknowledge, all those whose actions and lives bear testimony to this incredible blessing we have been given - the gift of Intuitive Intelligence∏™. That which keeps us connected to the Whole; with not just the right, but the *birth right* to become intuitively intelligent.

I hope that this book rekindles your inner power, ignites your great success and launches a connection to your own Intuitive Intelligence∏™, and by default, via your daily action, a connection to your own inner, greatness of Being.

# 1. SO WHY INTUITIVE INTELLIGENCE∏™?

"The subconscious is not limited by our imposed boundaries
of logic, space and time... It can transcend the ordinary to
touch upon a wisdom far beyond our everyday capabilities."

**Dr Brian Weiss**

Defying logic, have you ever wished that you had that
certain knack of making the right call? Has it ever
seemed like just as you are about to enjoy everything
you have ever worked for, it somehow blows up in your
face?  Or that if you have achieved the success you
always wanted, someone else has it just that little bit
sweeter...? If this is you, or some part of you, then
you're about to change all that.

Why? Because of a well-kept secret throughout the
years, which I've learnt to call Intuitive Intelligence∏™.
In fact, I was so convinced of its' existence, that I was
willing to be mocked and ridiculed for it, while being
tested and challenged by its' elusiveness.

Perhaps the most important thing about Intuitive
Intelligence∏™ is that it is always there for you. Like a
lifelong friend that is often ignored or taken for granted,
it never wavers in the hope that one day you will stop,
turn around and listen to its' subtle whisper. That's
what literally happened to me many years ago...

On the crisp, clear morning of 29 April 1985, I was on

my way home in a taxi cab after admitting my mother into the local hospital. She had spent the night wracked with the pain of cancer, and her body had simply had enough. Once she was settled in and comfortable at the hospital, I promised I would return with a 'home cooked' meal and a change of clothing. It was a short trip back home, but just as I prepared to climb out of the cab onto the sidewalk, I distinctly heard a voice say: 'Go back, go back, now.' There was nobody else around but the cab driver and he was looking at me with the strangest expression on his face, as if to say, 'What are you waiting for? Go on girl, get a move on....' So, at considerable risk of being called crazy, I found myself saying to him, 'Take me back, take me back to the hospital.' I could no longer ignore the terrible feeling gnawing at the pit of my tummy.

I reached the hospital a few minutes later and dashed back to where my mother was admitted. Never could I have imagined the sight that met my eyes. I found my mother in the corridor, strapped to the trolley, about to be wheeled into surgery. The nursing sister had stopped just long enough to pick up some forms. It was long enough for me to get there.

My mother had taken a turn for the worse and was booked in for emergency surgery. No one could have known that, least of all me. Yet, it seems that somehow, something called Intuitive Intelligence∏™ already knew. And thanks to its' still voice, I got to see my mother alive, one last time.

That single defining moment has since replicated into thousands of others throughout my life, where the inner voice of Intuitive Intelligence∏™ has never failed to guide me on point, second by second, time after time. It is like having a wise, old elder at your shoulder, ready to mentor you on call. Provided you listen. And you can have the same, except that your wise, old elder, is none other than your very own Intuitive Intelligence∏™. The ultimate core best part of you...

By the end of this book, you will learn how to use your Intuitive Intelligence∏™ to benefit every single aspect of your life, from your entrepreneurial career to your business; from your health and fitness to your wealth and financial freedom. Why is this so?

Simply because, as long as there is breath in your body, you have the right to become intuitively intelligent. Provided it is honoured and ethically used, your Intuitive Intelligence∏™ is accessible to you whenever you choose to call upon it. In short, simple steps, this book shows you how to make intuitively intelligent, effective decisions whenever you need to, so that you can live your ultimate successful life. You see, my personal mission is to spread the message of this hidden treasure worldwide. The message is that your Intuitive Intelligence∏™ is your *birth right.* Own your birth right, so that no matter who you are, you can live the life you *knew* you were meant to live.

# 2. WHAT'S THE DEAL WITH INTUITIVE INTELLIGENCE∏™?

*"If every great idea owes its' birth to intuitive thought, every great innovation owes its' birth to Intuitive Intelligence∏™."*
**Dr Manj Subiah**

So, what is Intuitive Intelligence∏™?

Before another word is written, Intuitive Intelligence∏™ is *not* intuition. In fact, it is much more than intuition, IQ, and EQ. To put it simply, it is an integral part of a much bigger picture. Only when four basic pieces of the puzzle come into synch in the human psyche, is Intuitive Intelligence∏™ fully present. So, what are these four 'pieces'?

Prior to my *informal* research from 1985, a period of intense *formal* research into Intuitive Intelligence∏™ began in 2003. During this time, one of my activities was to conduct interviews with leading Top 100 Company CEO's and senior executives. What became clear from the results was that they were able to manifest their largest, most ambitious intentions not only if they became very clear about what they wanted to achieve, but also if their intentions had a clear value and benefit to others in the company. In other words, if they clearly perceived that what they were doing would

5

benefit the lives of countless others as well as themselves, their subsequent actions would readily manifest into reality. In the culmination of results, it appeared as if they were co-creating with the Universe. In this mutually beneficial and cooperative choreography, they displayed four clear aspects to Intuitive Intelligence∏™: a heart, gut, head and cosmic aspect.

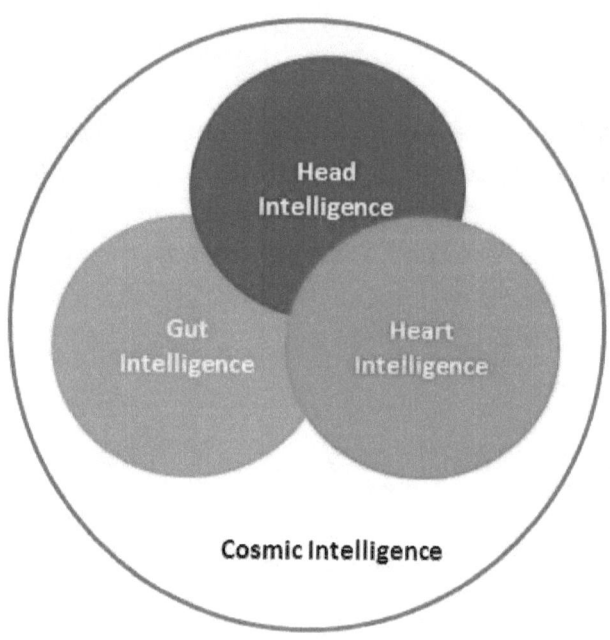

**Four aspects of Intuitive Intelligence∏™**

These four aspects of Intuitive Intelligence∏™ each break down into its' own components (explored further in the training programme). In terms of the actual intelligence context and process, the input or information received from the four aspects are interpreted and made sense of, by the person - the entrepreneur in this context. That information is then used to solve problems and guide effective decision making in the world - a criterion of intelligence.

In other research studies, the heart has been referred to as a 'brain' and so has the gut. Evidence shows that both heart and gut are remarkable in their ability to *know* that certain information was coming their way. In fact, studies showed that living things actually know what sort of information was coming, *before it happens. This was similar to what I had experienced.* Since then, I've encountered countless others who have learnt how to listen to their Intuitive Intelligence∏™. More and more evidence in terms of the interconnectedness of living things has come to light. For example, in astounding research by F.A. Popp (1994), the connectivity of living organisms was empirically demonstrated. Research studies also show how, in certain species, there appears to be an instinctual sense which triggers an alert in the event of impending danger, something which research subjects had no way of knowing prior to the event itself, (McCraty, R. et al., 2004). Still, further research demonstrates how communication between organisms was possible even down to the smallest species, like algae (Chang, J.J, et al., 1995). These and other studies show clear evidence that living species are able to 'signal' or communicate to one another.

All of this suggests the presence of an invisible cosmic connectivity which appears to include us - the human species. The greater implication of this is startling, in that it suggests that we may have access to this interconnected network, or cosmic Intelligence, particularly when we learn to use our own Intuitive Intelligence∏™.

**What makes up Intuitive Intelligence∏™?**

Besides the four aspects which make up Intuitive Intelligence∏™ (heart, gut, head and cosmic aspect), intuition per se, is but one single component of the entire Intuitive Intelligence∏™ composite. For practical purposes, only the four main aspects of Intuitive Intelligence∏™ will be discussed in this book.

What the heart knows, including ('emotional intelligence') brings its' own knowingness to the fore. What the gut knows, ('gut intelligence') allows for gut feel and gut instinct to come into play. What the brain knows ('brain intelligence') brings the past, present, new facts and knowledge to bear upon the situation. Lastly, cosmic intelligence links in the wisdom of collective consciousness. When these four flow in-synch in the person, it would not be inconceivable for a quantum leap of transformation, creativity, and innovation to take place. Add to this the faculty of instant sense making and wordless understanding, and the context for Intuitive Intelligence∏™ would appear to be set. Given the research done on the exceptional abilities, characteristics and performance of certain business leaders, this is no small deal.

There are three commonly understood intelligence criteria. **D**evelopment, **A**bility and **P**erformance, (Sternberg, 2000), and research shows that Intuitive IntelligenceΠ™ has these three criteria. In terms of development, Intuitive IntelligenceΠ™ has been shown to have the ability to grow and develop. Picture your five year old self. Very different from yourself at forty, fifty, or sixty, right? Common sense dictates that the Intuitive IntelligenceΠ™ of the five year old cannot compare with the tried and tested Intuitive IntelligenceΠ™ of the fifty year old. It has developed and evolved, along with the levels of awareness and individual consciousness. According to research, Intuitive IntelligenceΠ™ appears to develop and manifest in the performance and ability of the individual.

Within the business context, Intuitive IntelligenceΠ™ aids real time, high stake performance (the second intelligence criteria). The stakes are high here, as senior executives and CEO's are held personally accountable for their performance. In daily practice, there is little luxury of certainty for the leader and entrepreneur.

Ability, the third criteria of intelligence, is also used to demonstrate intuitively intelligent outcomes in business scenarios. Disturbingly, in some cases, an apparent lack of Intuitive Intelligence∏™ in prominent business leaders, may raise questions in the minds of peers. The same predicament may face entrepreneurs. For example, those that live in preference to their cognitive 'head' space may display a predisposition to delay decision making until all the bits and bytes of information come in. Peers will be heard to say: 'He/she just can't seem to make a decision.' On closer examination, though, that snap judgment may be premature. It is not that there is an inability to make an effective decision. More to the truth, it seems as though they are processing the information in an iterative, closed loop in their heads. The risk is, until they learn the process of using Intuitive Intelligence∏™ to make effective decisions, they risk becoming fixated or at the very least, stuck in this endless loop. The processes and tools given here as well as in the training programme help them break out of that trap into Intuitive Intelligence∏™ decision making and action mode.

In stark contrast to the former, 'stuck' state, is the dynamic developmental life cycle of Intuitive Intelligence∏™. The development and practice of Intuitive Intelligence∏™ results in an upward spiral which *evolves* and *involves* a conscious effort on the part of the individual. The initial awareness of a 'something other' or a sense of 'something beyond words' distinguishes Intuitive Intelligence∏™ from the usual thought patterns of the person. This development and practice manifests in the ability and performance of the individual. The dynamic life cycle which follows, shows how conscious effort and continual learning on the part of the person, sets up the upward spiral of Intuitive IntelligenceⲦ™ as it develops through practice and learning. The assessment of Intuitive IntelligenceⲦ™ is addressed in the second Handbook of Intuitive IntelligenceⲦ™ for Leaders.

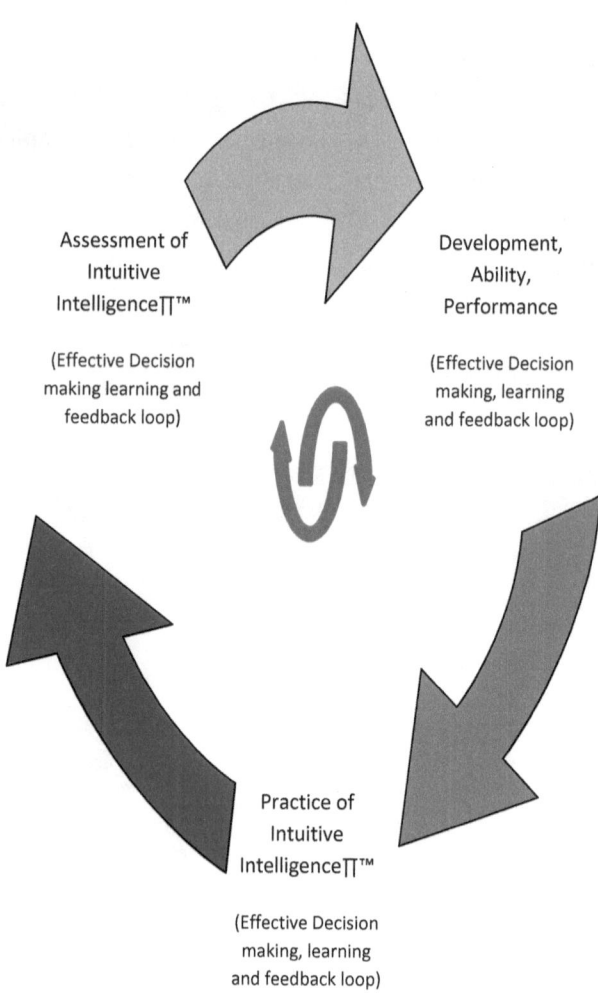

Assessment of
Intuitive
Intelligence∏™

(Effective Decision
making learning and
feedback loop)

Development,
Ability,
Performance

(Effective Decision
making, learning
and feedback loop)

Practice of
Intuitive
Intelligence∏™

(Effective Decision
making, learning
and feedback loop)

**The Life Cycle of Intuitive Intelligence∏™**

Research studies have shown that those who lived in preference to their heart space have a predisposition to act on impulse. Emotion may be a leading or underlying driver. Those that act in preference to their gut space displayed a predisposition to act in spite of the environmental information. Very rarely were they able to un-fixate and act counter intuitively. Intuitively intelligent leaders however, were able to process the information in their head, heart and gut, take cognizance of a cosmic aspect, put it all together in sense-making mode and then were able to make decisions and act effectively. In other words respond in synch with their Intuitive Intelligence∏™. This is a useful skillset for entrepreneurs as well.

As an exploratory research concept, it is useful to think of Intuitive Intelligence∏™ as an evolutionary intelligence accessible to humans. An intelligence which develops and has inherent in its' nature, the link and alignment with cosmic intelligence. Interestingly, way back in 1977, Carl Sagan was already proposing that we think of intuition and cosmic intelligence as evolutionary; something we humans can aspire to (Sagan, 1977). Intuitive Intelligence∏™ appears to be that cognitive bridge. A rather huge deal for us humans.

Interesting too, is research on business leaders, and various servant leader concepts which show that successful leaders are able to put aside petty ego promptings and subjugate self-interest, making ecologically sound decisions for the company, as well as the surrounding community. On a macro scale, such leaders can be seen to take decisions which benefit mankind as a whole. This pattern would match that of intuitively intelligent leaders acting in synch with cosmic intelligence. So, what's the problem?

The problem is that people all over the world have fallen into the trap of making disastrous decisions based on impulse, emotion, or unchecked intuition. Daily, in the news, you see or hear of road rage, blind shooting rampages, bombings, people killing, maiming, murdering, or being killed, maimed or murdered. People go so far as to harm their loved ones by their words or actions. The awful danger occurs when actions are based on decisions which show a total disregard for the four aspects of Intuitive Intelligence∏™. How do you stop such action from wreaking untold harm and suffering?

*In other words, how do you make really sound, effective decisions not just in business but in life?*

Start by simply UNDERSTANDING the core four aspects of Intuitive Intelligence∏™. When you understand this you set up an intentional and experiential AWARENESS dynamic within yourself. Then, by PRACTISING the processes and tools in this book, you similarly set up an upward spiral to develop your Intuitive Intelligence∏™.

What happens then?

Well, the process is that when all four aspects of Intuitive Intelligenceπ™ are in synch, whatever is held as a clear  intention shifts from the space of the possible to the physical. There are inherent criteria such as conscious effort, learning, consistency, ability and time; but it is possible to shift from intention to reality in terms of effective decision making.  A detailed process of decision making is included in the training programme. Before making an important decision, do an inner visual scan of your decision to ensure that all four aspects below have been duly considered.

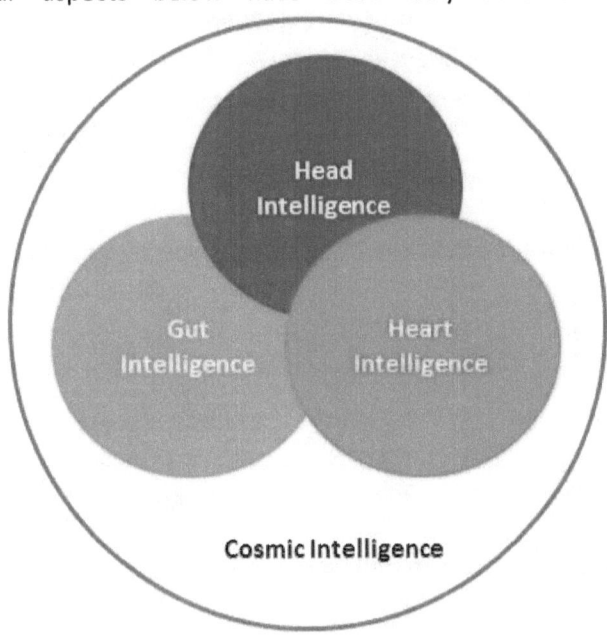

**Four aspects of Intuitive Intelligenceπ™**

# 3. HOW TO GET 'IN FLOW' WITH YOUR INTUITIVE INTELLIGENCE∏™

> *"One must simply observe the thoughts. When one does this, just as bubbles arise and dissolve into water, the discursive thought processes simply arise and dissolve in the mind.....Once this happens, there is a real opportunity to understand experientially...consciousness as 'luminous and knowing.'"*
> *Dalai Lama*

People pick up on how you come across and whether you are grounded in your own power or not. It is as subtle as a scent and as tangible as a touch. So, how do you ensure that you are in power and in flow with, your Intuitive Intelligence∏™?

Before we get to the how, there is one reason you end up losing your power and access to Intuitive Intelligence∏™. Actually, research shows there are a minimum of seven factors responsible for this, but let's focus here on the one which will get you the quickest turnaround in the shortest time. The remainder of the factors are covered in the training programme.

The short answer to how the loss of your natural flow occurred?

You permitted it. Yes, that's right. You permitted the

loss through the pattern of your thoughts and behaviour. Knowingly or unknowingly, you allowed yourself to shift into a space where a blockage (just like a kink in neural network piping) resulted in resistance to the flow of your Intuitive Intelligence∏™. While your Intuitive Intelligence∏™ was always there, ready to guide you...you just blocked it off with your set patterns of defence and resistance. The quickest way this shows up is when you just ignore or refuse to listen to your Intuitive Intelligence∏™. So, now that you know this, how do you get back into flow again?

Once you understand what happened when you blocked off the flow of Intuitive Intelligence∏™, you then become aware of your own underlying behavioural blockages. There are experiential processes in the programme to do this, but even at this cognitive level; once you really allow yourself an awareness of just what is happening inside yourself, that act of being present, moment by moment, without judging; allows Intuitive Intelligence∏™ to flow. Just like water flows, choosing the path of least resistance. You then start to become choicelessly aware of any pattern of resistance you have adopted and learn to release this and any other self-limiting beliefs about yourself, leaving the path clear once more for 'right action' to flow. Use the daily self-declaration: 'I am alert enough to get out of my own way, using my Intuitive Intelligence∏™ to achieve my outcomes.' In order to further help you get into flow, and stay connected to your Intuitive

IntelligenceΠ™, practice the 'RODE' process below whenever you feel disconnected and out of sorts.

**SIMPLE FOUR STEP 'RODE' PROCESS TO GET IN FLOW**

This basic four step process, 'RODE', means you can practice anywhere, anytime, to get into flow with your Intuitive IntelligenceΠ™. The key is to practice consistently. The steps are:

1. **R**elax your physical body through comfortable posture. Adopt a deep relaxed pattern of breathing. Now, even though you may use this process anywhere with practice; it may be practical in the initial stages, to do the process when you are alone and undisturbed. Else, you may find yourself explaining why tears are flowing down your face in the middle of a busy meeting. And just try explaining that you're not sad at all - that on the contrary, you're actually filled with joy and gratitude! You're bound to get some very strange looks!

2. **O**bserve with a sense of calm detachment your surroundings, and then focus on your breathing for five minutes; while asking yourself a simple question: 'Who am I.' Just observe what answer comes to mind and keep asking this question until you find the mind naturally subsiding into quietness. Feel a sense of this knowledge that *'you are Divine and strong in your own nature'*, whether you realise it or not. (Adapted from Sri Ramana Maharshi's teachings.)

3. **D**eclare in that space of silence between your

thoughts, your intention to be in touch with the current and flow of your Intuitive IntelligenceⲠ™. For example, "I am connected to my Intuitive IntelligenceⲠ™.' This clarifies your intention to be connected to a source of right action once more. That shows a choice to connect to a source of grace, power and great love. If you need an additional prompt, declare to yourself: 'My thoughts, words and deeds are guided by my Intuitive IntelligenceⲠ™.' Just be quiet after that intentional declaration, and notice the immediate sense of grace which floods your being. At this stage, do not be surprised when tears of gratitude flood your eyes. This is just an outward sign that you have connected completely with your Intuitive IntelligenceⲠ™.

4. Ease out of this state and gently bring yourself back to the present. Go ahead and carry out your day to day activities knowing that your actions are conducted within the power and flow of your Intuitive IntelligenceⲠ™.

Once you start to know and experience how to live, move, act and breathe in daily life within the current of your Intuitive IntelligenceⲠ™; the ebbs in your life are less, the peaks feel more natural, and pretty soon you are everything you hoped you would be and more...not just to yourself but to the world.

# PART TWO

# INTUITIVE INTELLIGENCEπ™ FOR ENTREPRENEURS

# 4. INTUITIVE INTELLIGENCETT™ AND THE ENTREPRENEURIAL MIND-SET

"Choose to master your mind, or it will master You."
**Dr Manj Subiah**

Perhaps the people who are at the most biting coalface of Intuitive IntelligenceTT™ are Entrepreneurs. If you are part of this 'do or die' group, you know from experience what it is like to trek alone through the terrain of indecision, gnawing self-doubt, challenge and cold rejection, every which way you turn. And yet, if you persist (and if you have gotten this far, you have); could the reason be that you maybe 'know' something that others don't?

Want the good news? This chapter is aimed at that part of you that *knows* better, no matter your present circumstances. The part of you that *knows* that you have your own unique pattern to share in this tapestry of life. This chapter is aimed at the entrepreneurial self - starter who is armed with a kernel idea, and wants to turn that into a profit generating machine. So, where to start...?

When Mind Power author John Kehoe and proponent Robin Banks, refer to the fifth law of mind power it points to the inner world of thought and the outer world of physical reality being interconnected. When we are grounded in an inner locus of control, while it may seem that things are not working in the outer world, we are nevertheless still able to function without falling to pieces. Failure comes from seeking success outside ourselves; a futile exercise. We cannot control the environment or other external factors, e.g. currency rates, stock markets, regulatory factors; other people's actions. If we allow other people or events to pull the rug out from under our feet, then we will be perpetually off balance. More painfully, that life lesson will recur until and unless we reclaim our inner locus of control and sense of balance once and for all. The laws of Intuitive Intelligence∏™ (described in the Handbook of Intuitive Intelligence∏™ for Leaders) will see to that. Getting connected to your Intuitive Intelligence∏™ is a way to stand strong in your natural power and flow. But how to start to swing things in your favor when everything seems to be falling apart? Let me share something that has worked for me without fail.

Practice a daily time of quiet meditation and gratitude first thing in the morning. Even if you just sit still for a moment, just observing your breathing, the pure value of this is simply to allow a certain mind-set to come into being, whereby your Intuitive Intelligence∏™ can generate a current which sets about going to work in your life. Since we already covered how gratitude is a driver in the process of developing your Intuitive

Intelligenceᴨ™; a good daily practice is to keep a gratitude journal. Often, in life we become resistant to the idea of our own greatness of Being. Gratitude is the number one force (besides love) that can shift that space, and allow our Intuitive Intelligenceᴨ™ and inner greatness to unfold out into the world. Picture the process whereby the Lotus flower blooms. Similarly this unfolding of inner beauty allows you to positively affect others by the ripples of your energy. In this way, your colleagues, customers, employees also get to experience and expand these ripples daily. Sales guru, Blair Singer, often references this daily entry into a gratitude journal with Alan Walters' Life Force Particles explanation, as one of the key ways of reclaiming 'lost' life force particles.

A successful mind-set also paves the way for winning responses. All entrepreneurs want to be successful, but few succeed. As discussed, the battle is often lost between the ears even before the first step is taken out into the field. So a winning mind-set needs a winning package to go along with it. Role models that you resonate with, help to inculcate some of the attributes of successful entrepreneurs. 'MEDS' is the acronym which captures the broad attributes of intuitively intelligent entrepreneurs. The advice is to top up on strong daily doses of it.

## 'MEDS' for the Intuitive Intelligence∏™ Mind-set

**1. M**ission mind-set: a mental framework of purpose fuelled by passion, consolidated by consistent practice focused on a clearly defined mission. Triangulate these three consistently: passion, purpose and practice until they build up a momentum of inner self - sustaining success toward your mission.

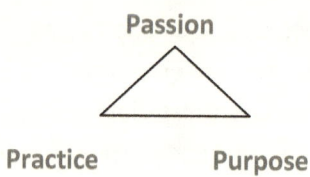

Passion

Practice          Purpose

**2. E**thics: a sense of not harming others, a sense of care and respect not just in the personal everyday way, but also in the formal business, duty and governance sense.

**3. D**iscipline: including the self-discipline to take necessary action no matter how hard it seems. Sometimes, this means defying the comfortable status quo in order to speak your truth. Something which, in itself, demands a fair dose of courage.

**4. S**ervice. Serve self and others through dishing up value with an abundance mentality. Again, this requires an inner locus of control and the ability to tell the difference between bias, intuition and Intuitive Intelligence∏™. More of this ability and skillset is covered in the training programme.

*Note to Entrepreneurs and Mentees:*

*'Think 100% focus." Identify what that project is for you and put your 100% thrust behind it.*

*"Have the 13 steps of Napoleon Hills's 'Think and Grow Rich' as part of your mind-set. Think big, dream big, leave a legacy. Have a purpose to provide value, and serve others. Be aligned in yourself so that there is no disconnect in your thought, word and deed or it will all unravel before you know it..."*

*In order to accomplish this you must have control over the thoughts in your mind.*

**SCRIPT TO SELF**

*1. How can I add value by this action?*
*2. How can I monetize this action? (Once off action)*
*3. How can I automate this action to keep on monetizing and adding value to others? (Repetitive action)*
*4. What difference can I make in the lives of my family, friends, company, country, planet...?"*

# 5. INTUITIVE INTELLIGENCEⱦ™ AND ENTREPRENEURIAL PURPOSE

*"Do you have a DEFINITE MAJOR PURPOSE, and if so, what is it, and what plan have you for achieving that purpose?"*
**Napoleon Hill**

The pain and quiet desperation of living a life lacking in clear, driving purpose is subtle, soul deep and destroying. It affects not only oneself, but everyone we come into come into contact with. Like stained money, a life lived without purpose is tragic, like a blueprint for success which lies ignored and trampled, in the dirt. It is the deepest insult, not just to oneself, but ultimately to the world. A world which needs the gifts you bear knowingly or unknowingly. Perhaps you've asked yourself why it is that success remains elusive for you? If so, take a look closer to home...

**So how to avoid the failure of living a life of unfulfilled purpose?**

**Follow the '3PC' process.**

1. **P**urpose of Self: Clarify what is your purpose in life? Some call that a terminal life or a legacy purpose. Something you would like to achieve before you die. Keep that as a second by second compass. Keep a clock nearby when you work. As you hear and see those

seconds tick by, you know, that's it. You're not getting a second chance, so what you do next has to stick. And if you want to make it count, here are the next steps...

2. **P**urpose of Business: What is your purpose as an entrepreneur? Some call it the business purpose or vision and mission of the business...This should be in synch with, not at odds with your Self purpose or it is dead before it starts. So, a fair amount of self-work needs to be done to get this part to a single distilled line. A key guideline to get to this point?

Keep a dream journal by your bedside and note down your dreams. During your quiet time, ask your Intuitive Intelligence∏™ to reveal your life purpose to you. These practices allow more and more information from the subconscious mind to surface. Intuitive Intelligence∏™ uses the subconscious as a vehicle to connect to the conscious part of you. A crucial element to this is what shape or form does the picture of success take on for you? What does this picture look, feel, sound, taste like?

3. **P**lan: What is the **Business Plan** mapped to get you there? What are the financial, sales, marketing and operational plans and how often will these be reviewed? Know that achieving success in your entrepreneurial venture is not going to be an overnight process, but you need to applaud yourself whenever you take steps closer to your goal. The plan is where

you get clinical, practical and focused. Several action plans may need to be drawn up depending on the extent of the gap between your goal and present reality. Make sure your plans pass muster by using 'SMART' - another popular management tool. In order for plans to succeed, they need to be **S**pecific; **M**easurable, **A**chievable, **R**esults based, **T**ime based. Once your goals and action plans have received the necessary buy in, monitor progress by doing a:

4. **C**heck: Control systems which track your course, ensure your progress. Most common is a control system of 'Plan Do Review.' A system of monitoring and feedback; it allows for learning, feedback and follow up. Do not be afraid of negative feedback from others or your own inner critic. Just remember to back it up with the hard facts, extract the learning from it, and move on, knowing that by acknowledging the learning, you've just notched up your ability of Intuitive Intelligence∏™.

When levels of uncertainty are highest, the ability to access Intuitive Intelligence∏™ on call is a crucial skillset for entrepreneurs. Through learning and feedback (immediate, nonjudgmental, open and honest, feedback), the development of Intuitive Intelligence∏™ is initiated to ensure success in consistent, goal driven efforts. Use your deepening understanding of Intuitive Intelligence∏™ to embed the 3PC skillset into your fundamental business practice.

# 6. INTUITIVE INTELLIGENCEΠ™, ENTREPRENEURIAL POSITIONING AND PRACTICE
## SKILLSET 1 of 5

*"The gift of their expertise is that it allows them to have a much better understanding of what goes on behind the locked door of their unconscious."*          **Malcolm Gladwell**

This chapter takes a deeper look at how, as an entrepreneur, one deals with the crucial question of position and practice, linked to purpose. How would you like to be ideally positioned for success no matter what the shifting goalposts in your business? Do you think it will be useful to reinvent your business and learn new tricks to keep ahead of the pack?

A critical skill in doing this harks back to Rudyard Kipling, '…keep your head when all about you are losing theirs.' This is critical for you to 'do what you do best, wherever you are, and among whoever.'  If you keep focused on your daily practice, it matters not what chaos erupts around you. You will find, before you know it, that the state of being the best becomes natural, until your inner dialogue becomes 'It's just what I do….'

Apart from being the best in your business, the factor of being well positioned in your market is important to ensure that you are perpetually grounded in understanding and gaining competitive edge. Your practice is to get and keep customers, build new and lasting relationships based on trust, quality and service, generate profits and more than likely, blaze a trail for your peers. The key to competitive positioning is not just in using tried and tested business tools like SWOT, STEEPLE (tools readily available on Google) and competitor analyses. The key to niche positioning is to:

- Uncover your own natural flow, expertise and talent and passion driven purpose.

- Understand what the demand is out in your market.

- Turn that into a value offering which gets you into the practice of getting and keep customers, building new and existing relationships, generating profits and sustainable growth.

But how to get a proper, well positioned, competitive start?

Start with the clues in your own life. Perhaps there are things you have been doing consciously or unintentionally throughout your life. By accessing your Intuitive Intelligence∏™ you uncover for yourself what worked, and what felt natural for you, from what didn't. These often come up as themes in your life. You may have thought of these as personal. But if it provides value for others, it's business. For example, perhaps as far back as you can remember it may have been a source of secret joy to you to use whatever spare time you have to read a good book. Or perhaps it was to cook or bake for others whenever you felt good and wanted to share that feeling? In my case it was when I shared knowledge that helped someone feel better about themselves; helping them to do better in their lives and to *be* better versions of themselves. By the time I'd finished the session, if they were more grounded in their greatness that was my fulfilment, full-stop.

Somewhere in there, is a pattern set into your life, something which grounds you in your unique practice which will link later to your positioning. Find out what it is - whether it is to write, or to cook, to work with children or to tell a good story. Perhaps, it is to finally share your own story..? Whatever it is, if you find that you do something not so much for the reward of it, but because it's just 'in you to do it'; now is the time to consciously identify those patterns of behaviour and make them intentional. The reason for this is that intentional activity is powerful and builds momentum. If your goal is good, it is worth your effort. When you put mental and muscle action behind your intent and practice, you set up a field of energy around you which attracts success. Try and commit to the following exercises with an open mind, free of judgement, for the subject matter is probably the most important one you will ever tackle in your life... **you**. *So, ready...?*

## INTUITIVE INTELLIGENCE∏™ POSITIONING EXERCISE (THEMES)

In a relaxed space, make sure you will not be disturbed. Take a pen and a notepad - yes, good old fashioned pen and paper - and start to write down the answers to the following questions:

1. 'What are the main themes in my life?' Later on, you will discover a golden thread that weaves throughout your life even into the stories and events that make up your life... For example: 'I'm all about making a difference,' or 'I'm all about healing,' or 'I'm all about teaching.' In my case, given my space, 'I'm all about connecting to Intuitive Intelligence∏™ and helping others do the same.' It may help to ask, 'what do I enjoy spending my **T**ime on, what gives me **H**appiness, what do I enjoy spending my **E**ffort, my **M**oney, my **E**nergy, my **S**pace on? In other words, what are the **'THEMES'** running through my life?

Know that these **THEMES** are intertwined with your life purpose, passion, story and message. To discover these themes is to uncover your unique message, your life purpose, place and positioning, upon which you can base your best practice. Make a note of the answers that come up. When you do this, you have just made the path of entrepreneurship that much smoother for you.

**2. Breathe** deeply and ask yourself: 'Who am I?' Keep on going with that question until you get beyond the superficial responses of the mind. For example, 'I am Sam, so and son's wife, or husband, father, mother,' etc. Go beyond all the roles you play in this world... Go beyond that to a space inside you where you can feel your own sense of Being. Breathe.... It may not come on the first try, but know that your inner space is there. It is what you are connecting with...that space where your mind falls silent and you start to feel yourself regain your sense of self power, something you may have long forgotten... All this is taking place inside you on a subtle, deep and dynamic level.... Breathe and sink into yourself. Allow at least 2 minutes to pass. Remain in that space quietly, gently. Feel a presence of love in that space. It has always been there, you just needed to reach out to it, and allow yourself to connect once more to your Intuitive Intelligence∏™. Now, in that silence, ask yourself:

**3. Ask**, 'Why am I here?' and take mental note of the answers that come up. Keep going, probing further still...

**4. Ask**, 'What is my purpose?' Do not be concerned if you don't get an answer right away. You are asking the question at a much deeper level so the mind takes time to search for that deeper level answer.

**5. Note** it down. Once you have the answers, record this in your notebook. You may call it a mission log or journal. Revisit this daily.

This daily practice is so that you can keep track of your progress along this path and avoid being stuck, while remaining grounded in shifting sands and goal posts. The entrepreneurial path is one less travelled, and your own toolkit needs to be fully replenished within yourself, before you help others out in the world.

# 7. INTUITIVE INTELLIGENCEΠ™ AND ENTREPRENEURIAL MARKETING SKILLSET 2 OF 5

*"Master your market."*     **Roger Hamilton**

So why would you want to, not just understand, but lead an involvement in marketing your entrepreneurial ventures?

As the quote instructs, it is important, because, to ignore marketing is seal your fate. It means to die a slow, painful, irrelevant death as an entrepreneur. There is a traditional school of thought that says, 'put out a product, then test the market's response to it.' That same school of thought says that 80% of entrepreneurial effort goes into operations.  Then, there is another school of thought which turns all that on its' head; saying, 'first find out what the market wants, then go serve that need and provide value.' This means that the majority of your time and effort is taken up with marketing. Either way, you are responsible for results, no matter the approach you choose. I recommend the latter. If you consider the business constraints you face, like most entrepreneurs, such as a lack of resources, lack of funding, lack of extra hands, no one to delegate to, lack of skills, technology, know-how; then marketing is not to be ignored.

So what do you do?

While I cannot point out the exact way you choose, (by now you are intuitively intelligent enough to decide that one by yourself), here are a few key points to help you with your marketing. Let's call them the '3m' questions. If you can answer these in thirty seconds or less, you are on your way to being an awesome marketer.

## 1. Message

What is your message? Some folks call this your elevator pitch. In other words; can you tell someone without hesitation, just who you are, what you do, what value you provide and why you are the unique person that can solve their problem and add value to their business? Breakdown and define your message in terms of the following:

What is your personal message, what is your business message and what is your product or service message? Although your personal message is often the driver and passion behind the business; your personal brand is a distinct identity from your business and your product brand. It is important to differentiate those three entities in order not to become confused and fall into the trap of becoming all things to all people. This loses you competitive edge in the long term. So clearly define: 'What is my personal message; what is my business message; and finally what is my product or service message'. When this level of clarity is reached, define your message in terms of timeline. For example; 'what is my personal message to focus on for the next five years; the next year, the next six months?' Start with your life legacy message and work backwards in the timeline, so that the daily actions you take all fall in line with your life legacy message. Intuitive Intelligence∏™ can help you reach a powerful level of clarity on your message.

## 2. Market

What is your market and niche? For example, this book is meant for entrepreneurs ranging from young start-ups in their twenties and thirties, to folks from their forties onward; who are still discovering their passion, wanting a new lease on life, re-inventing themselves and bringing their experience to bear.

The market environment is much more complex than a single focus on customers and / or consumers. The **CRISEA** model of markets which follows, enables you to define your market clearly.

**Adapted from Christopher, M.P. and Ballantyne, D. (1991)**

**Customer / consumer market**

The customer / consumer market is important to define clearly and in as much detail as possible. There are people that even have a picture of a particular type of person or an avatar they are targeting in terms of their marketing efforts. Include new, existing and old customers and build brand loyalty by repeated contact. Grow your customers from supporters to firm advocates of your business.

## Referral markets

These are word of mouth referrals and this means an organic growth in your business which is built on the most powerful marketing: reputation.

## Influencer markets

Your business needs to take note of the legislative and governmental environment it operates in, and to use these markets as opportunities to get involved in and influence decision makers. For example, as an entrepreneur, you can get involved in your local chamber of commerce.

## Supplier markets

Supplier partnerships can be set up such that relationships are geared toward a total solution for the good of the customer. This ensures a win-win sustainable supplier relationship.

## Employee markets

Employees are the best face to face dynamic advertisement for the business. As an entrepreneur, you and your employees are the best message for your company. Quality service, customer experience, promises made and kept are critical in this equation.

**Affiliate markets**

Many affiliates operate in a competitively similar niche but they are still helpful in promoting your business. Since they work on a commission basis, it means that you take a cut in profits by using them. However, it also means that you end up growing your business.

The third step key in the '3m' process involves knowing your medium.

**3. Medium**

What medium are you using to advertise your message?

The medium needs to maximise the message. From static to dynamic, whether written, audio, visual, or multiple options in-between, the promotion of your message needs to ensure that consumers and / or customers consciously make a choice to your advantage. A well selected media choice means that you are free to work *on* your business instead of *in* it; leaving you free to develop the rest of your business.

## NOTE TO MENTEES

*'Providing customer value is always at the centre of the wheel on which these '6P's' turn.*

*1. Product / Service: Does it provide value?*
*2. Price points: Well researched?*
*3. Place: Best location (virtual and / or physical)?*
*4. Promotion: Well targeted, focused?*
*5. People: Quality people with expertise?*
*6. Processes: Quality driven?*

## SCRIPT TO SELF

*'I am grateful*

*that I provide*

*on-going value*

*and am richly rewarded for it.'*

# 8. INTUITIVE INTELLIGENCEΠ™ AND ENTREPRENEURIAL SELLING SKILLSET 3 OF 5

*"Without question, the better you are at selling, or convincing or negotiating, the more of the world is open to you in terms of wealth, opportunities and great relationships."* **Blair Singer**

As the quote above indicates, the heart of true entrepreneurship is about knowing how to sell. In fact, the life skill, if not the life blood, of any successful entrepreneur is the ability to sell and close the deal. It's said that one may be without a job, but if one has a product or service of value to others, and one knows how to sell, one is never without an income.

**Rules and Tools:**

So is it possible to outline some fairly fail-safe rules and sales processes? Having learnt from some of the great masters in the field including my mentor Blair Singer; author of Sales Dogs, there are; but one of my favourite rules is ABC.

**A**lways ...**B**e...**C**losing... (The deal)

However, such rules should always be tempered by the use of your Intuitive IntelligenceΠ™. When you do this, you ensure that closing a deal is based on sound decision making processes. This ensures that you won't find yourself in a situation where you trusted a guy (or gal) you shouldn't have, and did business with him (or her) in spite of receiving all your cues to the contrary. If that does happen, exit the relationship - quickly! You can see how closing a deal in that case may be quite detrimental to your health and sanity!

So, where to start to get you to a point where you are *in* Intuitive Intelligence∏™ *and* closing those deals?

Well, here is a simple streamlined process to get you going for gold. In short, get your '**ESP – PPP'** on. The 'ESP' part is a share I received from Justin Cohen, author and public speaker. The 'PPP' part developed later on.

**1. ESP: E**ye contact, **S**mile and **P**osture. Remember the contact should feel genuine for you and for the person. Not dodgy or dismissive. If this is an initial contact and it is appropriate, offer your elevator pitch. Do it in such a way that the person feels privy to your share. Be open, positive, and relaxed; it helps people ease up in your presence.

**2. Problem**: What problem are you there to solve? In his book, Sales Dogs, Blair Singer has a detailed sales cycle which covers this sales process comprehensively. Your basic elevator script is now tested, where you can show the client what difference you make and what value you provide. Include brief numbers to back you up. For example, mine is "I have twenty years' experience in training and development and have trained 830 learners in various business and personal development programmes. My specialisation, particularly over the last ten years, is the value of Intuitive Intelligence⫪™ in business. So, here is a suggestion on how I think your problem could be solved..."

**3. Prepare** prior to appointments or meetings. Research the company. Know what information you will need before-hand. Do you know the clients' product or service? Can you anticipate the need and position yourself to serve that need? In this way, your meetings become a deeper connected level of experience and value for both parties.

**4. Practice**: Don't baulk at having practice runs before major meetings. Review goals after the meeting to see how well you met your goals. How well did you receive and follow the prompts and cues from your Intuitive Intelligence⫪™? What worked, what didn't? Take note of any lessons extracted so that you are ready next time round.

# 9. INTUITIVE INTELLIGENCEᴨ™ AND ENTREPRENEURIAL DELIVERY SKILLSET 4 OF 5

*"Whenever we have something we are good at - something we care about - that experience and passion fundamentally change the nature of our first impressions."* **Malcolm Gladwell**

In terms of creating a cycle of good impressions, once you have done the self-work to get yourself in flow (chapter three), you are now in a position to create and maintain powerful first impressions in the mind of your client or customer. You've worked hard to get them interested, you've closed the deal, but now you have to delight them, and keep them delighted by delivering the goods, time and time again. *But how?*

Well, even if you have your script down pat, realise that if you want to get and *keep* prospects and customers happy, you're in the business of information mining. You need to be able to listen, learn, explore, question and problem solve. No matter what that script and presentation prescribed, be prepared to discard it all and just listen to your customer. Take the time to mine down deep for those nuggets of information which will give you clues to make that customer experience (the test of delivery), delightful.

I remember way back when I was first tasked to implement a turn-around strategy in a failing company. The service provider had several problems, but the major one was a loss of revenue of over a million in the region. With all the stuff I'd learnt from my MBA, I was confident I could turn things around. After all, that is what 'MBA's' did right - make money? Turns out, I did not need that degree after all. Over the next eight months, a critical tool that turned things around was so remarkably simple and effective, I've called it the 'DEEP.' So named from the time my eighth grade English teacher asked me to give my classmates lessons on 'how to *think deep'* in their essay writing. At the time I don't even think I understood what that instruction meant...all that stands out is the memory of those perplexed faces of my classmates, at my home after school, trying to follow my fervent instruction to *'Think deep...think deep...')* Poor mites probably left my home *deeply* hypnotised! Anyhow, years later, here is the core of thinking '**DEEP**' for delivery.

**1. D**elve deep. Mentally switch places with your customer and get to grips with the problem. Don't be afraid to ask those disturbing, uncomfortable questions. In this case, it was, 'We are such a big player in the market, how come we're losing money? *Why*?' So the question had to be asked: *'Were we providing the kind of value that the customer wanted from us?'* Turns out that the uncomfortable but honest answer was 'No'. But we would never have gotten there had we not gone deep and asked those uncomfortable questions to begin with. And so, part of that successful turnaround was in making sure that the company delivered value aligned to what the *customer needed*, not what the Top Brass *thought.*

**2. E**xplore and explore again, the what, where, when, how and why of the problem. Only stop once you have the root cause /s nailed.

**3. E**valuate the various options or solutions to solve the problem. Weigh up the pros and cons of each option and eliminate those that are not the best fit solutions.

**4. P**lan of Action. Draw up a plan of action together with the client to get buy-in from the start or you will find that suddenly it is your plan and that *you* are responsible for the implementing it. So, if that is not what you actually signed up for, put a stop to it. Consultants and sales folk often fall prey to this. The client needs to own the problem and take responsibility for implementing the solution. A lack of accountability is not what you want to add to your problem list.

One of the traps facing entrepreneurs is not keeping grounded. Move at your own pace. If others are screaming way ahead of you, it matters not. You have to finish the game in your shoes, not someone else's. Don't make promises you cannot keep. Avoid being swallowed whole in your business. No matter how much money you make, that is a trap second to none and is just about the quickest way to flush the quality of your life away. Try to have regular time out sessions, even if it is to take daily, 'thirty minute - time-out sessions' to reflect. Look at options and ways in which you can have your business working for you instead of the other way around. Here are some ways to consider this.

- Try and think of ways to systemise your business. This sounds simple, but it depends heavily on the nature of the business and the sector it is positioned in. For example, a manufacturing environment versus a service environment will have very different ways of business systemisation.

- How dependent is your business on manual input versus automation when it comes to productivity? How can systems and technology help to increase profits?

- How much can you digitise your business to save time and money? For example, autoresponders allow proper follow up on your sales prospects, saving you time and money. They also increase sales conversions by building a relationship with your customer. Automation also involves setting up an online sales centre or virtual shop, depending on the nature of your business.

Remember that the nuts and bolts of quality delivery is not just about your product or service being first time right, on time. It is also about how you left that customer feeling about your product/ service and your company. Also try to translate that thinking to how y*ou feel about your business, and the value you* bring to make profits repeatable, assets usable, and growth sustainable in the long term.

# 10. INTUITIVE INTELLIGENCEπ™ AND INNOVATION
## SKILLSET 5 OF 5

*"They concentrate upon the known factors (the finished part) of the invention, and create in their minds a perfect picture of the unknown factors (the unfinished part) of the invention."*
                                                **Napoleon Hill**

While the opening quote takes us into the throes of someone innovating and inventing, let's first take a look at the overall picture of innovation. What does successful innovation or invention mean for an entrepreneur?

Sometimes, successful innovation requires a departure from the status quo, to the new, in order to create a product, service or process of value in the world. At other times, it is to repurpose existing technology for new applications. Still further down the timeline, it means to make a quantum leap and discover something we never knew existed in the first place, and then to put that to good use in the world. So, innovation can be of two main types; radical and incremental. History sometimes reminds us that both these types can appear in the same innovation at different stages. Take electricity for example. While it was a radical invention at first, the incremental innovations that it lead to were vast, such as toasters, electric kettles, electric cars.

Hence innovation means different things to different people. But what sets off the spark of innovation in the first place?

For entrepreneur Peter Wood, innovation was ignited by desperation. Direct Line Insurance, formed in 1984 was born out of his sheer necessity for a source of income.

For James Dyson, inventor of the vacuum cleaner; the irritation of a 'no-suction' problem on a Saturday morning was the impetus. He noticed that even when he'd emptied out the bag; it still didn't suck because the little suction holes were blocked. Shocked and surprised, that observation lead him to making a product with full suction all the time.

What drove them? In most cases, the mental gnawing pain of a problem seems to provide the fuel for their Intuitive IntelligenceΠ™ and their innovation. Some think of themselves as 'makers of things.' Still, others think of themselves as problem solvers, explorers, mavericks, heretics, and rebels in thought. There is however, a common thread...

**What do all innovators have in common?**

1. They learnt to act in the face of the unknown.

2. They were able to turn their great ideas into reality with action.

3. They made technology work for them, with an early instinct that technology was vital.

4. Their timing to invent and 'take to market' was superb.

5. Their effective decision making was critical.

6. They admitted their mistakes and learnt from them.

So, in a sense, throughout their lives, they knowingly or unknowing got very good at being *intuitively intelligent.*

In the opening quote, Napoleon Hill described a process used by inventors and innovators remarkably aligned to that used by business leaders pondering on a problem. A similar process used to stimulate Intuitive IntelligenceΠ™ is described below.

**Process of Problem solving using your Intuitive intelligenceΠ™: (PPAWI)**

1. **P**roblem vetting: Get clear on what you know about the problem and what you do not know about the problem. Make a list or a mind map if need be.

2. **P**icture in your mind the perfect outcome. This is the result or solution you are seeking.

Although at this stage you have no clear route on how to get to the solution.

3.  **A**sk yourself the question: 'If I already knew all I needed to know in order to get to this solution (complete perfect picture), what would I be doing?' Relax and clear your mind by just focusing on your breathing.

4.  **W**rite down those ideas as they pop up.

5.  **I**mplement the ideas once you've sifted through them.

## Note to Entrepreneurs

The difficult thing with most entrepreneurs is to admit mistakes; not to get defensive. Also, when taking on risk, it is to make sure that the downside is controllable. Another trick is accepting that 90% of everything ever learnt was by making mistakes and learning from them. But the real excitement is to realise that when you've learnt from your mistakes, it really means that you've notched up your Intuitive IntelligenceΠ™ that much more. Nike and 3M are good examples of role model companies which have embraced a culture of learning and ongoing innovation.

Check that your idea works first before you start borrowing money for it. Nobody pays you for a good idea, unless you own the product from a good idea. When you practice the processes, tools and techniques in this book, your entrepreneurial journey will take on an upward spiral. This is not to say that you will not hit a brick wall. You will. That is partly the point. When you do, though, your intuitively intelligent self will respond very differently from your old self. You will now respond in a sense to, either go over it, around it, tunnel through it, or just blow it out of the way completely - figuratively, of course.

When it comes to your entrepreneurial path, with fundamental, good business practice to support you, awesome role models behind you, and your *Intuitive IntelligenceⴥT™* to guide you, success cannot fail you.

# RESOURCES

## ACKNOWLEDGING THE WORK OF GIANTS

Agor, W.H. 1989, *Intuition in Organisations: Leading and Managing Productively*, Sage Publications; Texas.

Agor, W.H. 1989, "Intuition & Strategic Planning: How Organizations Can Make Productive Decisions", *The Futurist,* vol. 23, no. 6, pp. 20.

Barnard, C.I. 1936, *Mind in Everyday Affairs: An Examination into Logical and Non-logical Thought Processes.* Cyrus Fogg Brackett Lectureship Series, Princeton University Press; USA.

Beach, L.R. 1996, *Decision making in the workplace: a Unified Perspective*, Lawrence Erlbaum Associates; New Jersey.

Burke, L.A. & Miller, M.K. 1999, "Taking the mystery out of intuitive decision making", *The Academy of Management Perspectives*, vol. 13, no. 4, pp. 91-99.

Chang, J.J., *et al.*, 1995, "Research on cell communication of P.elegans by means of photon emissions", *Chinese Science Bulletin,* vol. 40: pp. 73-79.

Christopher, M.P.; and Ballantyne, D. 1991, *Relationship Marketing,* Heinemann; London.

Clancy, K.J. 1990, "The Coming Revolution in Advertising: Ten Developments Which Will Separate Winners from Losers", *Journal of Advertising Research*, vol. 30, no. 1, pp. 47-52.

Crossan, M.M., Lane, H.W. & White, R.E. 1999, "An organizational learning framework: From intuition to institution", *The Academy of Management Review*, vol. 24, no. 3, pp. 522-537.

Dalai Lama, 2005. The Universe in a Single Atom, Broadway Books; New York.

De Bono, E. 2009, *Think! Before It's too Late*, Vermillion Random House Group; London.

Demartini, J.F. 2008, *The Gratitude Effect,* Stonebridge Books; South *Africa.*

Demartini, J. F. 2002, *The Breakthrough Experience,* Hay House; USA.

Duggan, W. 2007, Strategic *Intuition: the creative spark in human achievement,* Columbia Business School Publication; New York.

Eisenhardt, K.M. 1989, "Making Fast Strategic Decisions

in High-Velocity Environment", *Academy of Management Journal*, vol. 32, no. 3, pp. 543.

Eisenhardt, K.M. & Zbaracki, M.J. 1992, "Strategic decision making", *Strategic Management Journal,* vol. 13, pp. 17.

Emmons, R.A. 2000, "Is spirituality an intelligence? Motivation, cognition, and the psychology of ultimate concern", *International Journal for the Psychology of Religion,* vol. 10, no. 1, pp. 3-26.

Gardner, H. 1993, *Frames of Mind: The Theory of Multiple Intelligences*, 2nd ed., Fontana Press; London.

Gardner, H., Kornhaber, M.L. & and Wake, W. 1996, *Intelligence: Multiple Perspectives*, Holt, Rhinehart and Winston Inc.; Florida.

Gladwell, M. 2005, *Blink: The Power of Thinking without Thinking,* Allen Lane; London.

Glaser, M. 1995, "Measuring intuition", *Research Technology Management*, vol. 38, no. 2, pp. 43.

Gleason, D., Nkomo, S.M. & De Jongh, D. 2011, *Courageous Conversations,* Van Schaik Publishers; Pretoria.

Hill, N. 2003, *Think and Grow Rich,* Vermilion; London.

Jung, C.G. 1995, *Memories, Dreams and Reflections*, (translated by Richard and Clara Winston), Fontana Press; London.

Jung, D.I. 2001, "Transformational and Transactional Leadership and Their Effects on Creativity in Groups", *Creativity Research Journal,* vol. 13, no. 2, pp. 185-195.

Kahneman, D. 2011, *Thinking Fast and Slow,* Farrar, Strauss and Giroux; New York.

King, M.E. 2009, *'Corporate Governance'* interview with MervynKing.*http://www.mervynking.co.za/pages/publication.htm*. *Accessed March 2009.*

Klein, G. 2002, *Intuition at work: Why developing your gut instincts will make you better at*

Louw, L. & Venter, P. 2006, *Winning in the South African workplace,* Oxford University Press; Cape Town.

McCraty, R. *et al.,* 2004, "Electrophysiological evidence of intuition: Part 1. The surprising role of the heart.", *Journal of Alternative and Complementary Medicine*, vol. 10, no. 1, pp. 133-143.

McTaggart, L. 2008, *The Intention Experiment,* Harper Element; London.

Miller, C.C. & Ireland, R.D. 2005, "Intuition in strategic decision making: Friend or foe in the fast-paced 21st century?", *Academy of Management Executive*, vol. 19, no. 1, pp. 19-30.

Mintzberg, H. & Westley, F. 2001, "Decision Making: It's Not What You Think", *MIT Sloan Management Review*, vol. 42, no. 3, pp. 89-93.

Nkomo, S.M. 2003, "Teaching business ethically in the "new" South Africa", *Management Communication Quarterly*, vol. 17, no. 1, pp. 128.

Nkomo, S.M. 2009, *Research Process:* Meeting, discussion and input regarding qualitative methodology. Lynwood, Pretoria.

Ornstein, R. 1991, *The Evolution of Consciousness*, Prentice Hall Press; New York.

Patton, J.R. 2003, "Intuition in Decision", in *Management Decision*, vol. 41, no. 10, pp. 989-996.

Peat, D. 2001, *Superstrings and the search for the theory of everything,* Abacus; London.

Raman, V.V. 2003, *Tirukkural,* 2nd ed., Thamil Caiva Valar Manram; Gauteng.

Reynolds, S.J. 2006, "A Neurocognitive Model of the Ethical Decision-Making Process: Implications for Study and Practice", *Journal of Applied Psychology*, vol. 91, no. 4, pp. 737.

Sadler-Smith, E. & Shefy, E. 2007, "Developing Intuitive Awareness in Management Education", *Academy of Management Learning & Education*, vol. 6, no. 2, pp. 186-205.

Sadler-Smith, E. & Shefy, E. 2004, "The intuitive executive: Understanding and applying "gut feel" in decision-making", *The Academy of Management Perspectives,* vol. 18, no. 4, pp. 76-91.

Sagan, C. 1977, *Dragons of Eden: Speculations on the evolution of human intelligence,* Hodder and Stoughton; London.

Senge, P.M. 1996, "Leading learning organizations", *Training & Development,* vol. 50, no. 12, pp. 36-37.

Shipham, S. 2011, Meeting and discussion with the author, August 2011, Midrand, Gauteng.

Shipham, S. 2006, *Research Process:* Meeting Presentation slides and discussion, September 2006, Midrand Gauteng.

Singer, B. 2012, *Sales Dogs,* BZK Press; USA.

Singer, B. 2011, *Little Voice Mastery,* XCEL Press; USA

Sonenshein, S. 2007, "The Role of Construction, Intuition and Justification in Responding to Ethical Issues at work: The Sensemaking-Intuition Model", *The Academy of Management Review*, vol. 32, no. 4, pp. 1022-1040.

Spender, J.C. 2005, "An Overview: What's new and important about Knowledge Management? Building New Bridges between Managers and Academics", in: Little, S. and Ray, T. eds. *Managing Knowledge: An essential reader*. Open University, SAGE Publications; London, pp. 127-154

Sternberg, R. J. 2000, *Handbook of Intelligence*, Cambridge University Press; Cambridge.

Sternberg, R.J. 2001, "Why Schools Should Teach for Wisdom: The Balance Theory of Wisdom in Educational Settings", *Educational Psychologist,* vol. 36, no. 4, pp. 227-245.

Swami Rajeswarananda, 2006. *Thus Spake Ramana,* Sudarsan Graphics; Chennai.

Vanmikanathan, G. ed. 1985, *Periya Puranum: A Tamil Classic on the great Saiva Saints by Sekkizhaar*, Sri Ramakrishna Math; Madras.

Vest, C.M. 2005, *Educating Engineers for 2010 and Beyond,* NAE Massachusetts Institute of Technology; Boston.

Vos Savant, M. & Fleischer, L. 1990, *Brain Power,* Judy Piatkus Publishers; London.

Weiss, B. 2004. *Same Soul, Many Bodies,* Piatkus; London.

# TESTIMONIALS

*What people are saying about Dr Manj and the
impact of Intuitive Intelligence on their lives...*

*"Dr Manj Subiah's groundbreaking work
has discovered how you can access your
own Intuitive Intelligenceπ™ in order to be
in the right place at the right time, doing
the right things." Blair Singer : Author of
SalesDogs®, Team Code of Honor and Little
Voice Mastery, Rich Dad Advisor to Robert
Kiyosaki.*

*"This book is a 'must read' for
entrepreneurs. It will ignite their Intuitive
Intelligenceπ™ and give them that
important 'insider' competitive edge." Dr
Hendrik Cronje, CEO, LeadAfrika*

"Dr Manj is all about Intuitive Intelligenceπ™." *Jill Wright, Denver, CO.*

"Manj, your words will inspire and flourish." *Dr John Demartini, USA*

"I am looking forward to the release of the book and seeing the results spread around the world like wild fire. Phenomenal human being!" *Johan van der Vyver, Cape Town, SA*

'I came in with a little knowledge about work and humanity but I came out with enough knowledge to last me a lifetime.' *Moses Maseko, SA*

"...this is an awe inspiring programme... it will change your life forever. You must *attend...Dr Manj has a higher purpose to serve others."  Tracy-Lee Sydney – Smith, Gauteng, SA*

*"Just love Dr Manj's commitment to the Intuitive Intelligence∏™ cause." Jayne Johnson, USA*

# ABOUT THE AUTHOR

Dr Manj Subiah is a #1 Intuitive Intelligenceπ™ proponent, author, key note speaker and transformational leader. She is a Cherie Blair Mentoring Women in Business Alumni, Accredited Enneagram Assessor and a mentor for the Mandela Washington Fellowship ('YALI'). Founder of Global Intuitive Intelligenceπ™ Systems, Dr Manj is a business advisor and entrepreneur with a drive to assist corporates and entrepreneurs in effective strategic decision making by means of innovative thinking, training programs, and keynote addresses on Intuitive Intelligenceπ™, peak performance of teams, self-transformation and self-mastery. Visit www.giis.co.za

www.ingramcontent.com/pod-product-compliance
Lightning Source LLC
Chambersburg PA
CBHW021008180526
45163CB00005B/1932